Security Forces Management Information System (SFMIS)

U.S. Air Force

The BiblioGov Project is an effort to expand awareness of the public documents and records of the U.S. Government via print publications. In broadening the public understanding of government and its work, an enlightened democracy can grow and prosper. Ranging from historic Congressional Bills to the most recent Budget of the United States Government, the BiblioGov Project spans a wealth of government information. These works are now made available through an environmentally friendly, print-on-demand basis, using only what is necessary to meet the required demands of an interested public. We invite you to learn of the records of the U.S. Government, heightening the knowledge and debate that can lead from such publications.

Included are the following Collections:

Budget of The United States Government
Presidential Documents
United States Code
Education Reports from ERIC
GAO Reports
History of Bills
House Rules and Manual
Public and Private Laws

Code of Federal Regulations
Congressional Documents
Economic Indicators
Federal Register
Government Manuals
House Journal
Privacy act Issuances
Statutes at Large

BY ORDER OF THE
SECRETARY OF THE AIR FORCE

AIR FORCE INSTRUCTION 31-203

29 JULY 2009

Security

SECURITY FORCES MANAGEMENT
INFORMATION SYSTEM (SFMIS)

COMPLIANCE WITH THIS PUBLICATION IS MANDATORY

ACCESSIBILITY: Publications and forms are available on the e-Publishing website at **www.e-publishing.af.mil.**

RELEASABILITY: There are no releasability restrictions on this publication

OPR: HQ AFSFC/SFOP   Certified by: A7S (Mr. David R. Beecroft)
Supersedes: AFI 31-203, 15 August 2001   Pages: 42

Military personnel who violate the provisions in paragraph 2.4 of this Instruction may be prosecuted under Article 92, Uniform Code of Military Justice (UCMJ), as well as any other applicable articles of the UCMJ or provisions of federal or state law. Civilian personnel who violate the provisions in paragraph 2.4 of this Instruction may be prosecuted under applicable provisions of federal or state law. Violations by military or civilian members may result in the full range of authorized administrative and disciplinary actions without regard to otherwise applicable criminal or civil sanctions for violations of related laws.

This instruction implements AFPD 31-2, *Air Provost Operations.* It provides guidance on general Security Forces duties and law enforcement operations. Security Forces Management Information System (SFMIS) use, to include new modules, is mandatory. Compliance with this instruction is mandatory and applies to Department of the Air Force military, civilian, Reserve, Air National Guard, personnel from other US military branches assigned or attached to Air Force units, contract Security Forces, and government-owned, contractor-operated (GOCO) and contractor-owned, contractor-operated (COCO) facilities. The terms "must," "shall," and "will" denote mandatory actions in this instruction. It is not necessary to send implementing publications to the higher headquarters functional OPR for review and coordination before publishing. Refer recommended changes and conflicts between this and other publications to HQ AFSFC/SFOP, 1517 Billy Mitchell Blvd Bldg 954, Lackland AFB, TX, 78236, on the AF Form 847, *Recommendation for Change of Publication,* through appropriate MAJCOM functional chain of command. Ensure that all records created as a result of processes prescribed in this publication are maintained in accordance with Air Force Manual (AFMAN) 33-363,

Management of Records, and disposed of in accordance with Air Force Records Information Management System (AFRIMS) Records Disposition Schedule (RDS) located at **https://www.my.af.mil/gcss-af61a/afrims/afrims/**.

This Publication requires the collection and or maintenance of information protected by the Privacy Act (PA) of 1974, in accordance with System of Records Notice (F031 AF SP B and F031 AF SP C). The authorities to collect and/or maintain the records in the publication are (10 United States Code (U.S.C.) 8013 Secretary of the Air Force: powers and duties; delegation by) The PA Systems Notice(s) is available at: **http://www.defenselink.mil/privacy/notices/usaf**

SUMMARY OF CHANGES

This instruction has been significantly changed and should be completely read through. A Table of Contents was added; Security Police was changed to Security Forces throughout this AFI; HQ USAF/A7S was changed to HQ USAF/A7SO throughout this AFI; 754th ELSS was changed to the 554th ELSG throughout this AFI; AF Form 3545A, Incident Report was added; background was revised to meet up-to-date information; defined Functional Review Board; defined Control Configuration Board; identified Headquarters Air Force Security Forces Center (HQ AFSFC)/Police Services as the SFMIS Systems Administrator; added director appointment of administrators and the signed appointment letter should be forwarded to HQ AFSFC; all wording changed from "will" to "should"; defined AF Form 3545A; defined Defense Clearance and Investigations Index (DCII); updated the Designated Approval Authority for SFMIS; merged Chapter 3 and Chapter 4; and created a new Chapter 4.

Chapter 1

POLICY AND PROGRAM MANAGEMENT

1.1. **Background.**

1.1.1. The Security Forces Management Information System (SFMIS) was developed primarily to meet the Congressionally-mandated Defense Incident-Based Reporting System (DIBRS) requirements and improve day-to-day operations of the Air Force Security Forces. It also provides statistical data for various users, and has grown to meet many other needs.

1.1.2. The SFMIS complies with DIBRS reporting criteria and provides the means to monitor and apply Air Provost and Integrated Defense selective enforcement measures. SFMIS also is useful for analysis of law enforcement statistics, as well as threat fusion. Future capabilities will be added to SFMIS through the HQ Air Force Security Forces Center (AFSFC) and Major Command (MAJCOM) Configuration Control Board (CCB).

1.1.3. Access to SFMIS by any personnel should be carefully scrutinized to ensure integrity of the system and protection of For Official Use Only (FOUO) and Privacy Act information.

1.1.3.1. IAW AFI 33-200, *Information Assurance Management,* the AFNetOps/CC approved access by foreign nationals to unclassified Air Force Information Systems (IS) where AFNetOps/CC is the Designated Accrediting Authority (DAA) or has delegated that responsibility. Before foreign nationals are authorized access and use of ISs, they must meet the requirements of AFI 31-501 and AFSSI 8522. This includes the AF provisioned portion of the Global Information Grid (GIG), (e.g. unclassified base LAN).

1.1.4. SFMIS users must know and ensure they meet the requirements of the Privacy Act of 1974 and report data only to those who have a valid need to know.

1.1.5. Criminal Activity Reporting. The SFMIS fully complies with the following requirements:

1.1.5.1. Report criminal activity to National Incident-Based Reporting System (NIBRS) per the *Uniform Federal Crime Reporting Act*;

1.1.5.2. Victim and witness notifications per the *Victim's Rights and Restitution Act of 1990*

1.1.5.3. Establishment of a central DoD database on domestic violence incidents per the *Lautenberg Amendment to the Gun Control Act of 1968*; and

1.1.5.4. Recurring requests for overall DoD law enforcement data.

1.2. **Responsibilities.**

1.2.1. The Office of the Under Secretary of Defense for Personnel and Readiness (OUSD (P&R)) develops overall policy for DIBRS and monitors compliance.

1.2.2. The Defense Manpower Data Center (DMDC) is directed by OUSD/P&R to keep a central repository of incident-based statistical data for analyzing trends in response to executive, legislative and oversight requests for information on criminal and high-interest incidents. DMDC created the data collection system to track and report DIBRS information from initial contact through investigation, prosecution, confinement and release. DMDC also reports NIBRS data to the FBI.

1.2.3. The Air Force DIBRS reporting process is triggered when law enforcement responds to a credible report of a criminal incident. If a crime is outside the jurisdiction of the Air Force law enforcement organization, DIBRS reporting is still a Security Forces responsibility for military members; however, jurisdiction/NIBRS reporting passes to the appropriate agency, such as Defense Criminal Investigative Organizations, FBI, or the local authority that has investigative jurisdiction of the case.

1.2.4. Active, Reserve and Air National Guard Security Forces units will comply with the reporting requirements mandated by Congress and outlined in DODD 7730.47, *Defense Incident-Based Reporting System (DIBRS)*, and DoD 7730.47-M, *Manual for Defense Incident-Based Reporting System (DIBRS)*.

1.2.5. AFSFC/SFOP is the Air Force Office of Primary Responsibility (OPR) for the SFMIS implementation and budgeting. SFMIS is funded through the operational budget of AFSFC.

1.2.6. AFSFC/SFOP is the functional lead for developing the SFMIS capabilities, by working with the MAJCOMs, via the CCB. AFSFC/SFOP:

1.2.6.1. Works with 554th Electronic Logistics Systems Group (ELSG) at Maxwell AFB-Gunter Annex, AL, to develop SFMIS and other Automated Information System requirements. (See para 1.2.11 for 554 ELSG responsibilities.)

1.2.6.2. Coordinates, once a month, or as necessary, with 554 ELSG to report DIBRS data to the DMDC.

1.2.6.3. Periodically reviews the system's usage to ensure compliance by all MAJCOMs and their respective units.

1.2.6.4. Directs corrective action on SFMIS errors.

1.2.6.5. Chairs Functional Review Board (FRB). The FRB consists of functional subject matter experts and meets to discuss the needs/future needs of SFMIS.

1.2.6.6. Chairs Configuration Control Board.

1.2.6.6.1. Brings AFSFC/SFOP and the Program Managers Office (PMO) together to prioritize/discuss the needs of SFMIS.

1.2.6.6.2. Grants access when notified in writing by a MAJCOM A7S Director of the appointment of a System Administrator (SA) at a MAJCOM.

1.2.6.6.3. AFSFC/SFOP is the overall SFMIS SA.

1.2.7. Each MAJCOM A7S should appoint a primary and alternate SA to grant permissions and access for the MAJCOM's units. No contractor is authorized to be an SA unless approved in writing by AFSFC/SFOP. MAJCOMs will provide a copy of appointment letters to AFSFC/SFOP, and a signed copy of the Global Combat Support System-Air Force (GCSS-AF) Form 41, *System Authorization Access Request*.

1.2.7.1. MAJCOMs are encouraged to send a representative(s) to the CCB meetings. Representatives should be able to discuss current and future SFMIS requirements.

1.2.7.2. MAJCOM SFMIS SAs should monitor units to ensure that reports of commander action on incident reports and traffic tickets are forwarded to DIBRS on a timely basis (commander's action completes the report for the DIBRS database).

1.2.7.3. MAJCOMs will not approve use of other automated programs as substitutes for existing SFMIS capability.

1.2.7.4. SFMIS operates through the use of role-based access, granted to authorized users at all levels in the System Administration Module. When notified in writing by the installation Security Forces commander, of the appointment of a SA at an installation, the MAJCOM SA will grant specific accesses and roles.

1.2.7.5. MAJCOM SAs should periodically review the use of SFMIS by the command's units and ensure everyone is using the system as required. Such reviews should also be considered during inspections and staff assistance visits. MAJCOMs are encouraged to develop checklists to ensure compliance.

1.2.8. Installation commanders must ensure all DIBRS-specified incidents, and reports of command action, are reported via SFMIS. This includes "internal" investigations which are NIBRS/DIBRS reportable incidents. For definitions of reportable incidents, refer to DoD 7730.47-M, *Manual for Defense Incident-Based Reporting System*. DIBRS-reportable incidents must be documented on an AF Form 3545A, *Incident Report,* or Report of Investigation, and reported to SF Admin and Reports or AFOSI. **Note:** Reports of Survey (ROS) are often related to the theft, loss, or damage of government property, which are also usually DIBRS reportable. An ROS can be added to an AF Form 3545, *Incident Report,* as an attachment. The purpose of an ROS is to determine if the person is accountable for the item and does not establish criminal activity. NOTE: AF Form 3545A, *Incident Report,* is a SFMIS generated incident report. An AF Form 3545, *Incident Report,* is used at locations where SFMIS is not available and a hard copy generated report must be completed using Word or IMT.

1.2.8.1. Only commanders designated on "G-Series" orders are authorized to sign the Command Action of the AF Form 3545A, *Incident Report,* or Report of Investigation. Unit Commanders or Section Commanders are the only personnel allowed to sign the Command Action area of the DD Form 1408, *Armed Forces Traffic Ticket.*

1.2.8.2. Local Security Forces units must verify with local agencies any Civil incarceration of military personnel on active duty to ensure DIBRS-related information is submitted via SFMIS.

1.2.8.3. Installation commanders must ensure command action on incident reports and traffic tickets is reported via SFMIS within the suspense set by the local Security Forces Administration & Reports Section or other activity, per AFMAN 31-201 Volume 7, *Security Forces Administration & Reports*, Chapter 1, para 1.5.3. Timely reporting of command action ensures compliance with DoDD 7730.47 and DMDC timelines.

1.2.9. Security Forces Unit Responsibilities.

1.2.9.1. The installation Security Forces squadron commander will appoint a Primary and Alternate SA. The appointment letter will be sent to the respective MAJCOM SA. No contractor is authorized to be an SA unless approved in writing by AFSFC/SFOP. If a unit feels they need more administrators, it will be requested in writing and considered on a case-by-case basis, with final approval coming from AFSFC/SFOP. SAs will act as the local grantors of roles and level of access for personnel requiring access to SFMIS. SAs will only have access to the SA module in SFMIS. They must create another account to have access to the other modules without SA rights. NOTE: Group accounts are NOT authorized.

1.2.9.2. The installation Security Forces commander will establish internal controls to allow management to view each DIBRS-reportable incident. Normally, the NCOIC, SF Administration Reports, Operations Superintendent, SF Investigations, Operations Officer and Commander are granted full access as reviewing and approving officials before the data is transmitted up the chain.

1.2.9.3. The installation Security Forces commander will ensure all DIBRS-reportable incidents are reported through SFMIS. The report of commander's action is of paramount importance to the Air Force's responsibility for DIBRS reporting. On a yearly basis, DMDC provides DoD with DIBRS data on criminal statistics. One of the major areas reviewed is commander's action reports. To ensure Air Force compliance, SF unit SA will conduct a monthly review of all pending cases and attempt to finalize them. An incident is not considered finalized until it's either adjudicated or determined no action taken.

1.2.9.3.1. SFMIS entries are also required for most Security Force responses requiring some type of action to be taken besides a standalone AF Form 1168, *Statement of Suspect, Witness, or Victim* (e.g. traffic violation, vehicle accidents, etc.)

1.2.9.4. The Security Forces Reports and Analysis (SFAR) section will establish a 60-day suspense for reports requiring commander action and place them in a suspense file. Annotate the suspense date on the cover letter of the report. If prior histories exist, print and attach the history to the report for the commander's information. (Note: Prior histories are normally provided only for suspects/subjects of the report.) If response on command action is not received by the due date, dispatch a letter, "Notice of Late Suspense" giving an immediate suspense. If a response is not received after 7-days, send a "Notice of Second Late Suspense" to the unit commander with a courtesy copy to the group commander. DFC can extend suspenses on a case-by-case basis.

1.2.9.5. On the first duty day of each month, each SFAR section will perform a computer run of the previous month's Criminal Summary Report. They will then task the Security Forces Investigations Section to compare that reporting with the local AFOSI detachment point of contact to ensure all Defense Clearance and Investigations Index (DCII) information is reported. DCII is a single, automated central repository that identifies investigations conducted by DoD investigative agencies and personnel security determinations made by DoD adjudicative authorities. This is done to ensure duplicate incidents are not entered into DCII and that all incidents are recorded as required. NOTE: DCII is an automated central index that identifies investigations conducted by Department of Defense investigative agencies. AFOSI is the agency that heads entry into DCII.

1.2.9.5.1. ANG units may run their reports on the first UTA of each month. This may be accomplished by the DFC appointed SFMIS monitor or that individual's alternate.

1.2.9.6. The DFC will ensure a copy of AF Forms 3545A, *Incident Report*, or the SFMIS Incident Report and criminal history, CVB Forms 1805, *Violations Notice*, are transferred to the local AFOSI detachment when reporting to DCII is required and copies are filed in the SF Administration & Reports filing system.

1.2.9.6.1. The local AFOSI may be satisfied with having the Criminal Summary Report in lieu of the AF Form 3545A, *Incident Report,* and Report of Investigation. The main objective is to ensure all DCII information is provided to the AFOSI officials.

1.2.9.6.2. Air National Guard and Air Force Reserve Security Forces units which are co-located on active duty Air Force bases will not run the Criminal Summary Report. They will forward the DIBRS-reportable information to the active duty host Security Forces unit, which will perform the computer run of the previous month's Criminal Summary Report.

1.2.9.7. Air Force Corrections. Each installation, whether they have a confinement facility or not, is responsible for entering inmate information into the SFMIS Confinement Module as well as reporting the case outcome to SFAR. The only exception is Air Force inmates confined in civilian facilities on civilian charge(s). The SF unit Corrections Officer or point of contact will ensure this entry has been completed on every member sentenced to confinement by a court-martial. NOTE: Personnel referred to USAF SF Level I confinement facilities must have the crime resulting in their confinement reported to DIBRS via SFMIS or AFOSI channels.

1.2.10. The AFNETOPS/CC serves as the DAA for SFMIS.

1.2.11. The 554 ELSG is responsible to design, acquire, install, integrate and support the information systems necessary to provide the Air Force with the right combat support information.

1.2.11.1. The 554 ELSG assists AFSFC in developing an Operational Requirements Document that will serve as the Statement of Work (SOW) for a SFMIS project. AF/A7S will be the final approving authority for new requirements.

1.2.11.2. The 554 ELSG utilizes contractors as necessary to meet Security Forces requirements.

1.2.11.3. IAW DoDI 8510.01 the 554 ELSG is responsible for appointing an Information Assurance Manager (IAM) for SFMIS. The IAM will be qualified IAW DODD 8570.1.

Chapter 2

REPORTABLE DISCIPLINARY INCIDENTS AND SECURITY

2.1. Defense Incident-Based Reporting System (DIBRS).

2.1.1. DIBRS is primarily a reporting system covering all active duty, reserve, and guard military personnel. Security Forces must input civilian data for those who commit offenses on Air Force installations into National Incident-Based Report System (NIBRS), which is the primary reporting system for all civilians.

2.1.2. For definitions of reportable incidents, refer to DoD 7730.47-M, *Manual for Defense Incident-Based Reporting System.*

2.1.3. The installation Security Forces commander will ensure all reportable DIBRS incidents are entered into SFMIS. DIBRS submissions must be completed by the 15th day of each month. DIBRS submissions pending final action, to include the report of commander's action, must be tracked until final disposition.

2.1.3.1. Units must correct DIBRS errors. The Security Forces commander can determine if this is the responsibility of the patrolmen, SFAR, SA, etc. SFAR must search for DIBRS errors at least monthly and attempt to correct entered errors. See Attachment 2 for some common DIBRS errors and corrective action.

2.1.4. The AF Form 3545A, *Incident Report,* or Report of Investigation, records the data reportable to the Defense Manpower Data Center (DMDC). Incidents not covered by DIBRS will be documented and reported under Uniform Code of Military Justice guidelines. The SFMIS-generated Incident Report Summary (AF Form 3545A) or an original AF Form 3545, is approved for use as the final file copy and to document, with original signature or digital signature, the Commander's Action.

2.1.5. The Air Force Board for Correction of Military Records is the only authority who can order SFMIS records be cleared; regardless of the outcome of the report and age of the offender.

2.2. National Incident-Based Reporting System (NIBRS).

2.2.1. NIBRS (Reportable for CONUS only) has the same responsibilities as outlined in section 2.1. NIBRS is comprised of 6 segments (e.g., Administrative Segment, Offense Segment, Property Segment, Victim Segment, Offender Segment, and Arrestee Segment) and 53 data elements.

2.2.2. Reporting requirements for civilian offenders are only required by NIBRS.

2.3. Security and Passwords

2.3.1. SFMIS is Common Access Card (CAC) enabled. In order to access SFMIS with your CAC card, it must be done through the AF Portal. The CAC card can only be associated with one user name. If multiple user names are required for your duty position then users will be assigned user names/passwords for access and permissions commensurate with "the need to know" information within the system. **Individual passwords will not be shared with other users.** It is a system security violation for multiple users to share the same user ID and password. Passwords will be changed at least every 60 calendar days, immediately upon compromise, or after 45 days of inactivity. SFMIS can identify the number of days remaining until a change of password is required.

2.3.1.1. Audits of the system will be done as warranted for proper accountability when there is a change in SA.

2.3.2. Should a lockout occur as a result of an improper or forgotten password, the MAJCOM or unit SA will assign a new password; however, the account will remain locked for a period of one hour or until the user's identity can be positively identified. Users who have expired accounts must have their passwords reset through the system administrator or 554 ELSG/Field Assistance Service (FAS) at DSN 312-596-5771/COMM 334-416-5771. MAJCOM SAs can perform this function for unit SAs. Unit SA's can perform this function for members of their unit. Problems encountered should be forwarded to the 554 ELSG/FAS for resolution. If a problem cannot be resolved within a reasonable time (24 hours), ensure the user gets a trouble ticket from the FAS, which will be forwarded to the SFMIS Program Managers office, until the problem is fixed.

2.3.2.1. If you have log-in problems due to your CAC please refer to local procedures to unlock your CAC card.

2.4. **Privacy Information.** All SFMIS data is protected by the Privacy Act and must be handled as For Official Use Only (FOUO). All information will be strictly controlled in accordance with AFI 33-332, *Air Force Privacy Act Program of 1974*, to ensure it is only released to officials with a need-to-know. **Individuals may access the SFMIS for authorized, official purposes only. Military members who improperly access SFMIS or its information, or provide or enable such access to third parties, for other than official, authorized purposes, may be punished under Article 92, Uniform Code of Military Justice (UCMJ), as well as any other applicable articles of the UCMJ or provisions of federal or state law. Civilian personnel who improperly access SFMIS or its information, or provide or enable such access to third parties, for other than official, authorized purposes, may be prosecuted under applicable provisions of federal or state law. Violations by military or civilian members may result in the full range of authorized administrative and disciplinary actions without regard to otherwise applicable criminal or civil sanctions for violations of related laws.**

2.4.1. All SFMIS users must be aware that data displayed on monitors may be susceptible to unauthorized viewing. Take appropriate action to ensure privacy data is always protected.

2.4.2. Protection can be enhanced by installing additional "time-out" features when the system is not being used, or installing "screen savers" at prescribed time intervals. The SA can assist in applying these features.

2.4.3. Violations of the system's operation or unauthorized release of the "FOUO" information will be immediately reported to the unit SA, who will notify the commander at each level of concern.

2.4.4. The installation Security Forces commander will coordinate with all base functions that may require access to SFMIS information. This will normally include Wing/Support Group Commanders, Staff Judge Advocate, AFOSI and Military Equal Opportunity staff. Access refers to information contained in SFMIS which SFAR can print out, not a user name/password. Personnel outside security forces who need live access to SFMIS should be given "read only" access with Security Forces commander's approval.   Other agencies should be carefully screened to validate a need to enter SFMIS and approved locally by the Security Forces commander.

Chapter 3

SYSTEM OPERATION

3.1. Hardware/Software Requirements.

3.1.1. SFMIS is a web-based product. It requires Internet Explorer 6.0 or higher. The system is password protected. SFMIS uses state-of-the art integrated software to ensure all data is properly encrypted for security and meets DoD Certification and Accreditation standards.

3.1.2. For best performance use hardware/software as recommended by DISA at Maxwell AFB Gunter Annex Alabama. *Note:* As technology advances and changes are made to accommodate future data, upgrading of peripherals may also be required. Should this occur MAJCOMs will be notified in advance.

3.2. SFMIS capabilities. This list is not all inclusive and more features are added with each SFMIS release. Currently, the SFMIS program has the following capabilities:

3.2.1. Case Reporting, Accidents, Tickets (principal module for reporting DIBRS).

3.2.1.1. Some capabilities include entering reports and citations, DEERS search, Suspension/Revocation/Debarment (SRB) Roster, case search and a history search.

3.2.2. Limited Confinement (to be DIBRS compliant).

3.2.2.1. Some capabilities include tracking DIBRS-reportable information, inmate release dates, pre-trial/post-trial confinement and victim notification.

3.2.3. System Administration.

3.2.3.1. Some capabilities include resetting passwords, creating accounts and adding roles. *Note*: If you have a SA account the only module you can access with the SA user name is the SA Module.

3.2.4. Pass & Registration.

3.2.4.1. Some capabilities include issuing visitor passes, Restricted Area Badges (RAB) and DD Form 2220 issuance, if used. (RAB module is not currently mandatory to use, due to the fact it cannot encode the magnetic strip for gate access).

3.2.5. Combat Arms

3.2.5.1. Some capabilities include inputting training requests, class assignment, course fired, AF Form 522 History and supply account.

3.2.6. Armory

3.2.6.1. Some capabilities include placing weapons/munitions/equipment in inventory, tracking weapon issues and the authority to bear arms, registration of Privately Owned Vehicles/Privately Owned Weapons (POV/POW).

3.2.7. Web-based Computer-Based (CBT) Trainer (available in release 6.0).

3.2.7.1. The primary capability is an Interactive step-by-step process for each module on SFMIS.

3.2.8. 'Oracle "Discover Viewer"'

3.2.8.1. The primary capability is searching for statistics which offers parameter setting for ad-hoc queries

3.2.9. MAJCOMs or units desiring additional capability must contact the SFMIS POC at AFSFC/SFOP, 1517 Billy Mitchell Blvd, Bldg 954, Lackland AFB TX 78236-0119, DSN 312-945-0266/5028.

3.2.10. AFSFC/SFOP periodically publishes SFMIS Newsletters. This information will appear on the SFMIS "Message of the Day," AFSFC's homepage and/or posted on the SFMIS Administrators and Users Community of Practice (on the AF Portal). These messages inform users of developments, new releases, and other important information. Users should check these sources for updates often, and are highly encouraged to submit items to AFSFC/SFOP for future publication.

3.3. **Assistance.** The FAS also provides assistance to Base Network Control Centers, Defense Mega Centers and users worldwide. New user accounts must be created by MAJCOM or local SA. The FAS is not empowered to validate authorized use.

3.4. **On-Line Manual.** The SFMIS program has an online help manual available for users. The manual is user-friendly and can be printed for easy reference. Refer to DoD 7730.47, *Defense Incident-Based Report System*, for the DIBRS/NIBRS code tables. *Note:* These code tables are subject to change. DMDC controls the additions/deletions on the code tables.

3.5. **SFMIS Training.** The installation Security Forces commander must ensure their personnel are trained to use SFMIS to meet their installation needs and DIBRS requirements. Training and familiarization should not be conducted using the SFMIS "live" system modules because of the potential for mistakenly reporting false information. To facilitate hands-on training at the MAJCOM and unit level, the SFMIS Training Site (DMZ) may be utilized. MAJCOM and unit SAs can request access to this training site by contacting the 554 ELSG Program Management Office. Do not contact the FAS for DMZ access. Once the MAJCOM or unit SA is granted access to the DMZ, user access can then be granted. The SFMIS DMZ can be accessed at **https://ser-0367-dmapp.saic.com/SFMIS5/**.

3.5.1. Computer-Based Training (CBT). The SFMIS CBT module provides familiarization and refresher training. It is the primary means for familiarization training. CBT can be found on the SFMIS homepage.

3.5.2. Mobile Training Team (MTT). Units may also request 554 ELSG to conduct a MTT to provide familiarization training at the requesting unit's expense. This training must be scheduled so it does not impact a SFMIS mission requirement or release. You can obtain this information on the SFMIS page or contact AFSFC/SFOP, DSN 945-0266/5028/Comm 210-925-0266/5028, or 554 ELSG/PMO DSN 596-5004/6700 Comm 334-416-5004/6700, for training assistance.

3.6. **Unresolved Matters.** SFMIS issues will be directed to AFSFC/SFOP, 1517 Billy Mitchell Blvd, Bldg 954, Lackland AFB, TX 78236-0119 or **afsfc.workflow@lackland.af.mil** for resolution.

Chapter 4

HANDLING OF SFMIS INFORMATION

4.1. **Requests for SFMIS Information.**

4.1.1. For requests for release of SFMIS information, follow AFI 33-332, *Air Force Privacy Act Program,* and DOD Regulation 5400.7/AF Supplement, *DoD Freedom of Information Act (FOIA) Program.* Individuals or agencies desiring copies of reports (to include enclosures) or Security Forces blotters will do the following:

4.1.1.1. If the requester desires copies of statements, they must submit a request under the *Privacy Act (*AFI 33-332) or the *Freedom of Information Act,* as required by DOD Regulation 5400.7, as supplemented.

4.1.1.2. Insurance companies requesting case reports concerning clients will make the request in writing. Units will assess a fee per DOD Regulation, 7000.14-R, Volume 11a, *Reimbursable Operations, Policy and Procedures.* Company checks will be used and made payable to Base Finance and mailed to the local SFAR office. Turn over checks to Finance using DD FM 1131, *Cash Collection Voucher.* No fees are assessed to private individuals requesting information on incidents they were involved in unless copies exceed regulatory amounts. Consult DOD 7000.14-R for further guidance.

4.1.1.3. Police or government agencies (e.g. Drug Enforcement Agency, Recruiters, Family Advocacy) requesting information for official reasons will receive all requested information after the identity of the agency can be verified. Such requests must be made either in person upon proper identification or using official letterhead. The written request can be mailed or faxed. Ensure the requester is advised to include points of contact, mailing addresses and phone or fax numbers to ensure a prompt response. Ensure requesters are authorized release under the Privacy Act (AFI 33-332) before disclosing the information. The requester's letter will be attached to the case files/blotters for a matter of record. Responses can be mailed or faxed back. Maintain a log to verify action was completed.

4.1.2. If the government was involved in an incident or the situation might result in litigation against the government, consult the Staff Judge Advocate before release of any information.

4.1.3. Statistical information may not be released without AFNETOPS/CC approval. This does not prevent Installation Commanders/DFCs from using their own statistics to obtain criminal patterns or brief personnel on criminal activity in the local area of their installation. Statistics will not be released for unit, numbered AF, regional, or MAJCOM comparisons. While local commanders may desire this information for comparison purposes, this does not meet the System Security Access Agreement's requirement for a valid "need to know" in order to release SFMIS information. Improper release of information without a valid need-to-know may jeopardize continued SFS access to the SFMIS. Contact AFSFC/SFOP for additional guidance.

4.1.4. All SFMIS users are required to read their responsibilities of safeguarding SFMIS information and sign acknowledging these responsibilities. All units will keep on file the acknowledgement of responsibilities for personnel within their unit. A copy of the responsibilities of safeguarding information along with the acknowledgement of responsibilities can be found on the SFMIS CoP>SFMIS Supporting Documentation>Account Generation Documentation.

4.2. Adopted Forms.

AF Form 847, *Recommendation for Change of Publication*

AF Form 3545(A) *Incident Report*

GCSS-AF Form 41, *System Authorizations Access Request*

DD Form 1408, *Armed Forces Traffic Ticket*

AF Form 1168, *Statement of Suspect/Witness/Complaint*

CVB Form 1805, *Central Violations Bureau Violations Notice*

LOREN M. RENO, Lieutenant General, USAF
DCS/Logistics, Installations & Mission Support

Attachment 1

GLOSSARY OF REFERENCES AND SUPPORTING INFORMATION

References

DoDD 7730.47, *Defense Incident-Based Reporting System (DIBRS)*, 15 Oct 1996

DoD 7730.47-M, *Manual for Defense Incident-Based Reporting System*, 25 July 2003

DOD Regulation 5400.7-R/AF Supplement, *Air Force Freedom of Information Act Program* April 2006

DOD Regulation, 7000.14-R, Volume 11a, *Reimbursable Operations, Policy and Procedures* May 2001

Lautenberg Amendment, *Firearms Prohibition and Domestic Violence Convictions*, amendment to the *Gun Control Act of 1968*

Section 534, United States Code, *Uniform Federal Crime Reporting Act* Jan 04

Sections 10606 and 10607 of Title 42, United States Code, *Victims Rights and Restitution Act of 1990* Jan 2004

Section 922 of Title 18, United States Code, *The Brady Handgun Violence Prevention Act* 2008

AFPD 31-2, *Air Provost Operations*, 10 April 2009

AFI 33-332, *Privacy Act Program*, 29 Jan 2004

AFMAN 33-363, *Management of Records*, 1 Mar 2008

AFMAN 31-201V7, *Security Forces Reports and Analysis*, 21 Jan 2002

Air Force Records Information Management System (AFRIMS)

Abbreviations and Acronyms

AFOSI— Air Force Office of Special Investigations

AFPD— Air Force Policy Directive

AFSFC— HQ Air Force Security Forces Center

AFVA— Air Force Visual Aid

BDOC— Base Defense Operations Center

CBT— Computer Based Training

CCB— Configuration Control Board

COCO— Contractor Owned Contractor Operated

DCII— Defense Clearance and Investigations Index

DEERS— Defense Eligibility Enrollment Reporting System

DFC— Defense Force Commander

DIBRS— Defense Incident-Based Reporting System

DMDC— Defense Manpower Data Center

DoD—- Department of Defense

DoDD—- Department of Defense Directive

DoDI—-Department of Defense Instruction

DRMO—-Defense Reutilization Management Office

FOUO—-For Official Use Only

FRB—-Functional Review Board

GOCO— Government Owned Contractor Operated

GSA—-Government Services Administration

IAM—-Information Assurance Manager

JDET—-Joint Drug Enforcement Team

MAJCOM—-Major Command

NIBRS—-National Incident-Based Reporting System

OPR—- Office of Primary Responsibility

PMO—-Program Management Office

ROI—-Report of Investigation

ROS—-Report of Survey

SA—-Systems Administrator

SF—-Security Forces

SFAR—- Security Forces Administration and Reports

SFMIS—- Security Forces Management Information System

SJA—-Staff Judge Advocate

SRB—-Suspended, Revocation, Debarment

SSAA—-System Security Authority Agreement

TTPG— Tactics, Techniques, and Procedures Guide

UCMJ—- Uniform Code of Military Justice

VWAP—-Victim Witness Assistance Program

Attachment 2

COMMON DIBRS ERRORS AND CORRECTIVE ACTION

A2.1. Introduction:

A2.1.1. This attachment contains common errors associated with the monthly Defense Incident Basted Reporting System (DIBRS) to the Defense Manpower Data Center (DMDC) and corrective actions which should be taken to correct them.

A2.2. Common Mistakes Causing Errors

A2.2.1. The mistakes listed here have the potential of causing several different types of errors or prevent the record to be transmitted.

A2.2.2. Check DIBRS/NIBRS Buttons as Required

A2.2.2.1. When users are entering in reports, they need to refer to the offense tables to determine when these buttons need to be checked to comply with congressionally mandated reporting requirements.   After receiving the results from the April 2008 submission and researching the cause of these errors; users still have many cases erroneously unchecked despite this requirement. SFMIS has help documentation to assist users in identifying which cases have reporting requirements.

Figure A2.1. NIBRS/DIBRS Codes – A.

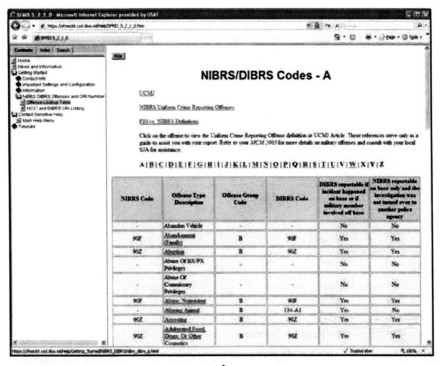

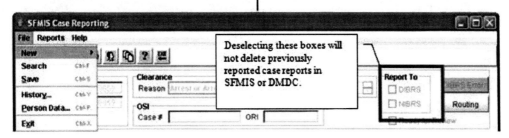

A2.2.3. Improper Routing of Case

A2.2.3.1. As illustrated below, users need to ensure they properly route cases.

Figure A2.2. Routing Button.

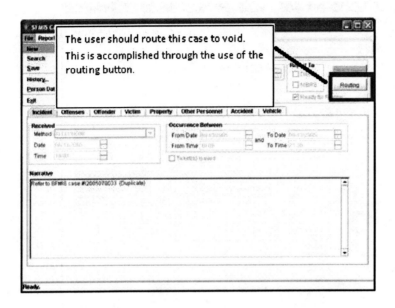

A2.2.4. Specific Error Types and Recommended Corrective Action

A2.2.4.1. **A604** *If Category is AA (Arrestee), Arrest/Citation Number is required*

A2.2.4.2. This   error   message   informs   the   user   when   an   offender   is
apprehended/detained, a date must be entered.

Figure A2.3. Apprehension Information.

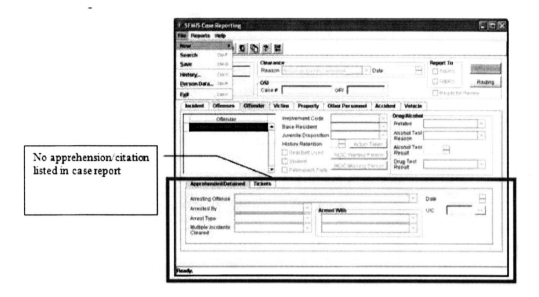

No apprehension/citation listed in case report

A2.2.5. **A606** *If Category is AA (Arrestee), Arrest/Apprehension Date is required*

A2.2.5.1. This error message informs the user when an offender is apprehended/detained, a date must be entered.

Figure A2.4. Date of Apprehension.

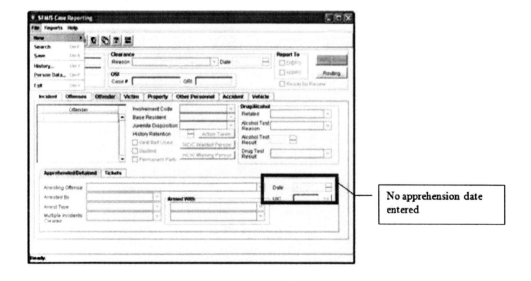

No apprehension date entered

A2.2.6. **A608** *If Category is AA (Arrestee), Arrest Type is required*

A2.2.6.1. This error message informs the user when an offender is apprehended/detained, the type of arrest must be indicated in the case report.

Figure A2.5. Arrest Type.

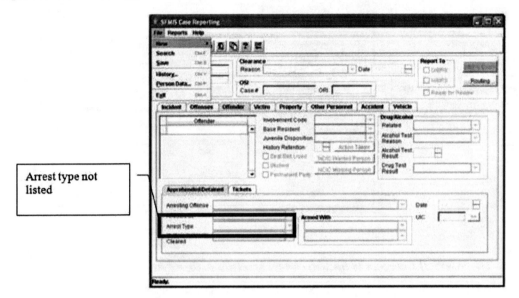

A2.2.7. **A617** *If Category is AA (Arrestee), Sex of arrestee is required and must be either M or F*

Figure A2.6. Gender Identification.

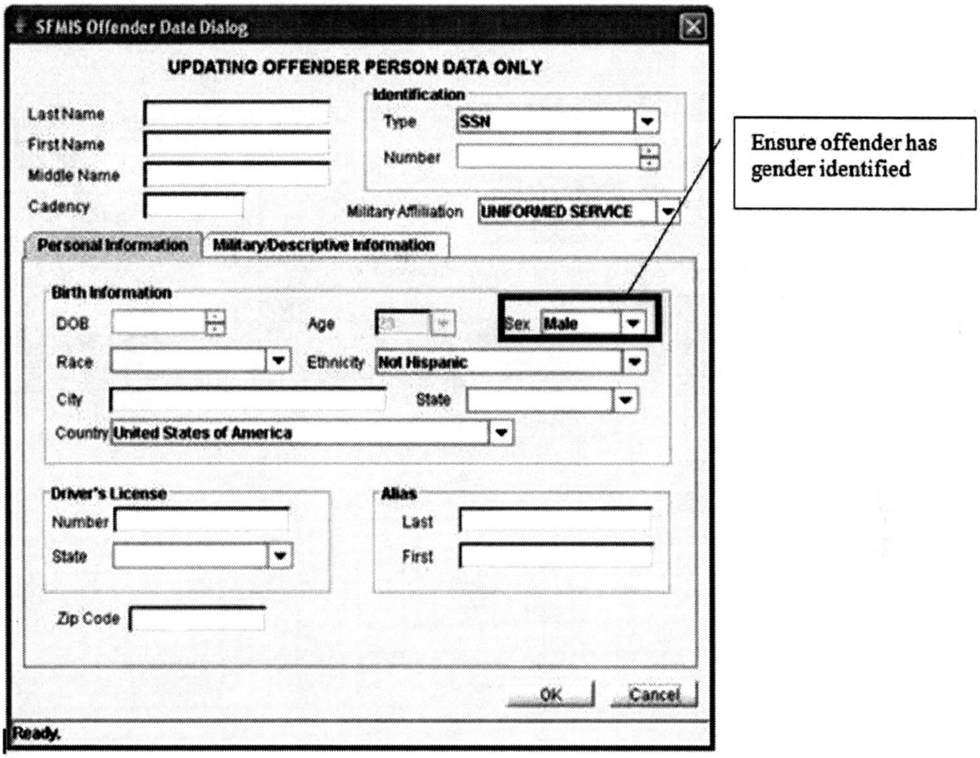

A2.2.8. **A647** *If actual Age of Arrestee is less than 18, Disposition of Person Under 18 is required*

Figure A2.7. Juvenile Disposition.

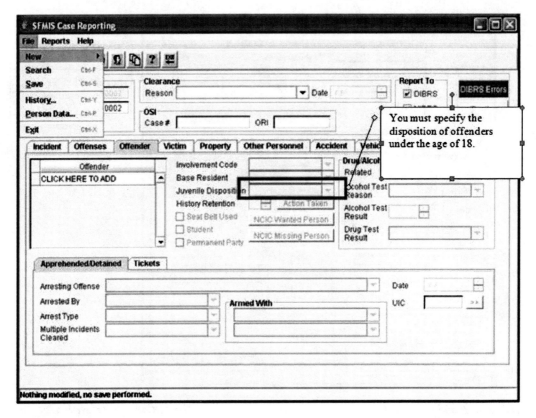

A2.2.9. **A802** *Personal information (last name, first name) is missing from Offender/Arrestee Report segment.*

A2.2.9.1. As shown in the figure below, SFMIS will generate a person identification number for unknown persons. However, if a record is reported to DMDC in this state it will cause an error.

A2.2.9.1.1. **Scenario 1:** User enters information indicating an apprehension took place, when in fact one did not take place. If an apprehension did in fact take place the offender record needs to be updated accordingly.

Figure A2.8. DIBRS Box.

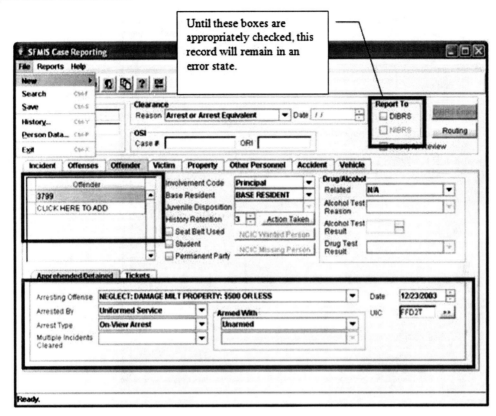

A2.2.9.1.2. **Scenario 2** : Upon opening up the offender record (by double clicking the name of the offender – not the person icon, which opens the person dialog), several cases do not have complete names. For example, the offender record has a first and middle name but not last name in the record.

A2.2.10. **A806** *SSN/Alien Registration (Field 71) should be provided when SSN/Alien Registration Designator (Field 70) is present in Offender/Arrestee segment.*

A2.2.10.1. In the Apr 2008 submission all 806 errors were from OS bases on foreign nationals. However, they were listed as family member/dependents. Further research needs to be conducted on whether or not these people are issued SSNs.

A2.2.11. **A810** *Both SSN/Alien Registration Designator (Field 70) and SSN/Alien Registration (Field 71) should be provided in Offender/Arrestee segment if non-"00" Offender ID exists.*

Figure A2.9. Identification.

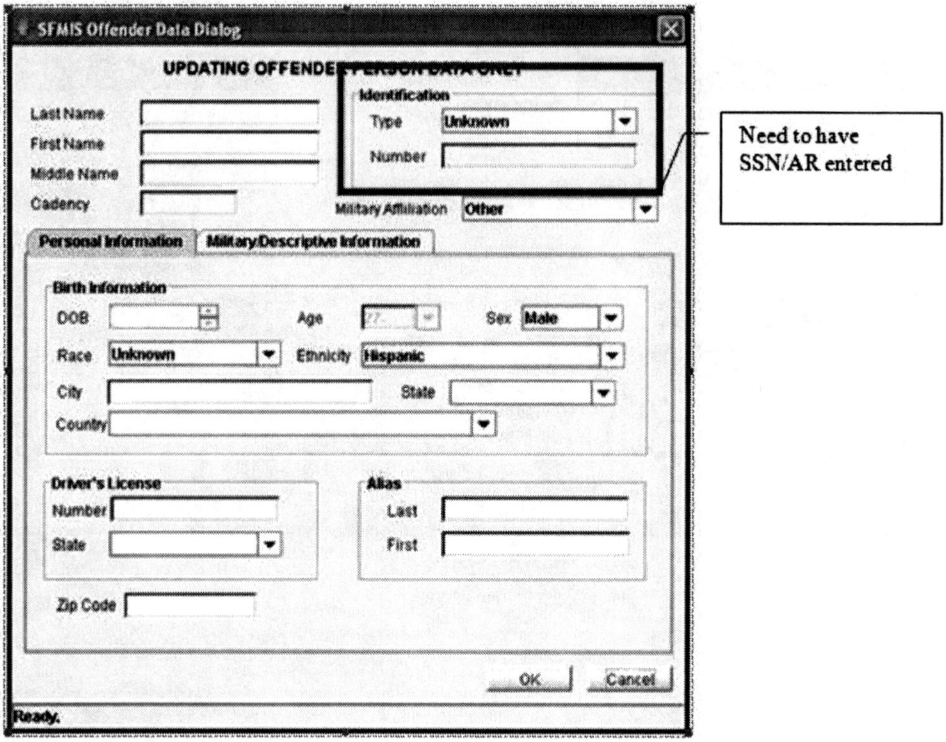

A2.2.12. **D514** *Transaction attempted to process a segment for which no parent incident (segment M) exists*

A2.2.13. This error message informs the user when SFMIS attempts to submit a commander's action record which there is no longer a case report for. This is most likely caused by different record retention periods required by the USAF and DMDC. SFMIS maintains case reports for five years, at which time the records are purged as required by the Air Force Records Management System (AFRIMS), unless Brady Law or other requirements apply. DMDC does not have a purge requirement at this time. These differences cause these types of errors which may require manual correction by the SFMIS Program Management Office (PMO).

A2.2.14. **D576** *For Sanction Type AU, field 106 (Sanction Amount) is required*

A2.2.14.1. This error message informs the user when an entry into the commander's action record and the sanction (field 106) states fines (AU) have been imposed, the amount of the fine must be included.

Figure A2.10. Fines.

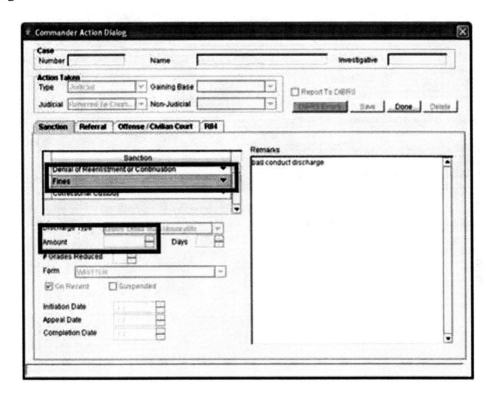

A2.2.15. **D577** *For Sanction Types AH, AV and AW, Sanction Days is required*

A2.2.15.1. This error message informs the user when an entry into the commander's action record and the sanction (field 106) states a delay of promotion (AH), extra duty (AV), or restriction (AW) has been imposed; the number of days must be included.

Figure A2.11. Length of Restriction.

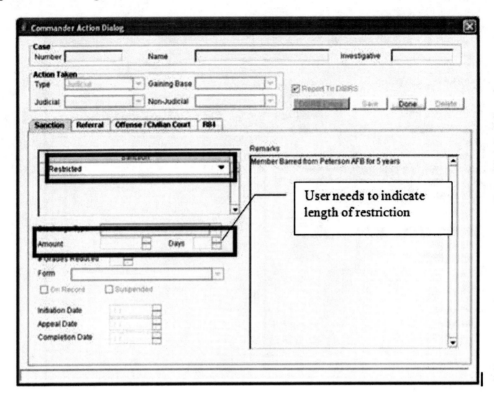

A2.2.16. **D780** *Warning: Missing Offender/Arrestee segment for Commander's Report segment (orphan D segment exists)*

A2.2.16.1. This message informs the user they need to ensure the commander's action record matches the case record. Also, ensure that the commander's action record is complete. For example, if you have an "Administrative" action taken against the offender, select the applicable sanction(s).

A2.2.17. **D801** *Personal information (last name, first name) is missing from Commander's Report segment.*

A2.2.17.1. This error messages informs the user there is an error with offender's name in the commander's action. The example shows the error due to the offender's name not being complete. This information must be corrected in the offender record, and the person record should be reviewed.

Figure A2.12. Name.

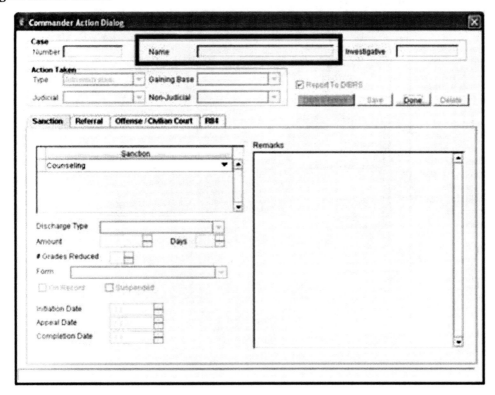

Figure A2.13. Personnel Record.

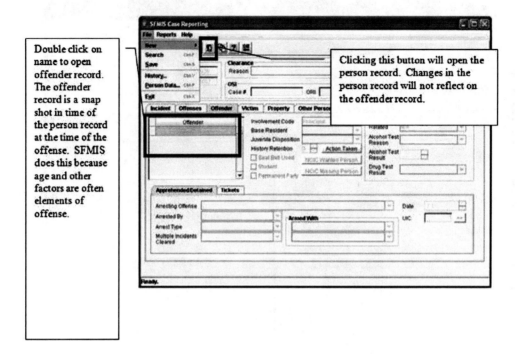

Figure A2.14. Whole Name.

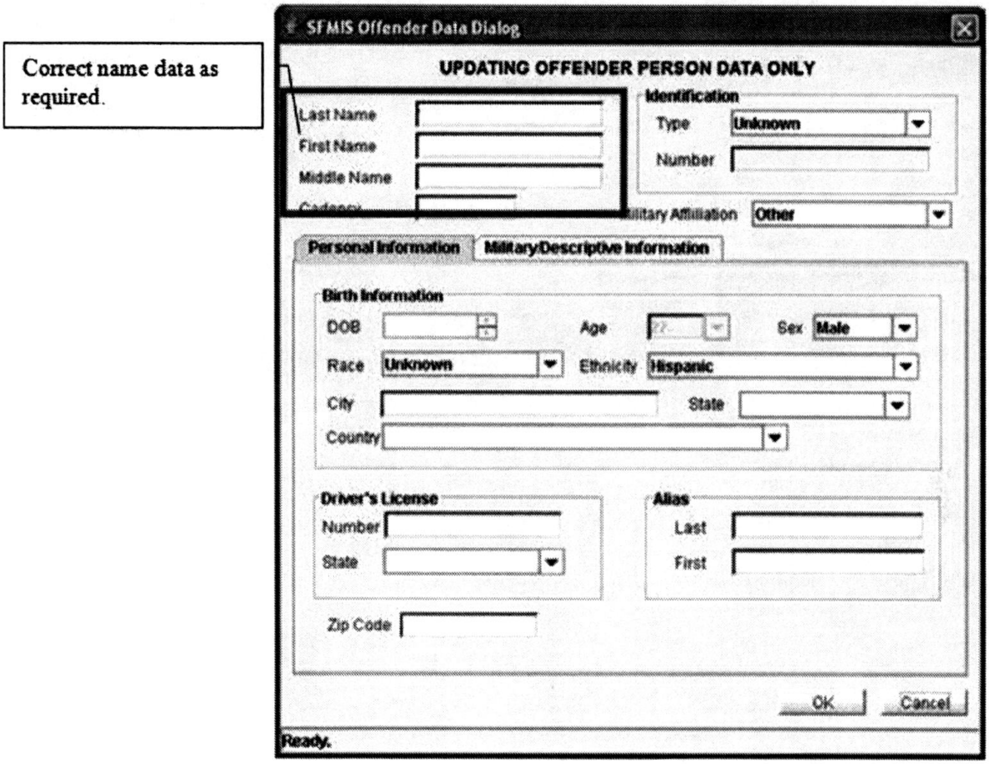

A2.2.18. **D815** *Personal information (last name, first name) is missing from Commander's Report segment.*

A2.2.18.1. This error informs the user an offender's name is missing or does not match the case report. In this example you will note the offender names do not match it the Incident Report and the Commander's Action Record. Once reported to DMDC, this will cause an error. Users need to correct the information as outlined in D801.

Figure A2.15. Offender.

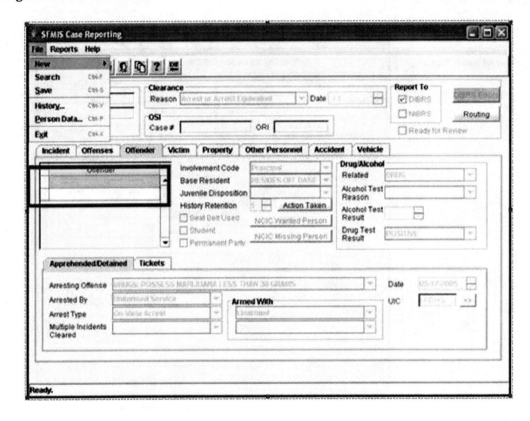

A2.2.18.1.1. The offenders listed in the above and below figures should match. Since the names do not match, DMDC reports an error.

Figure A2.16. Name.

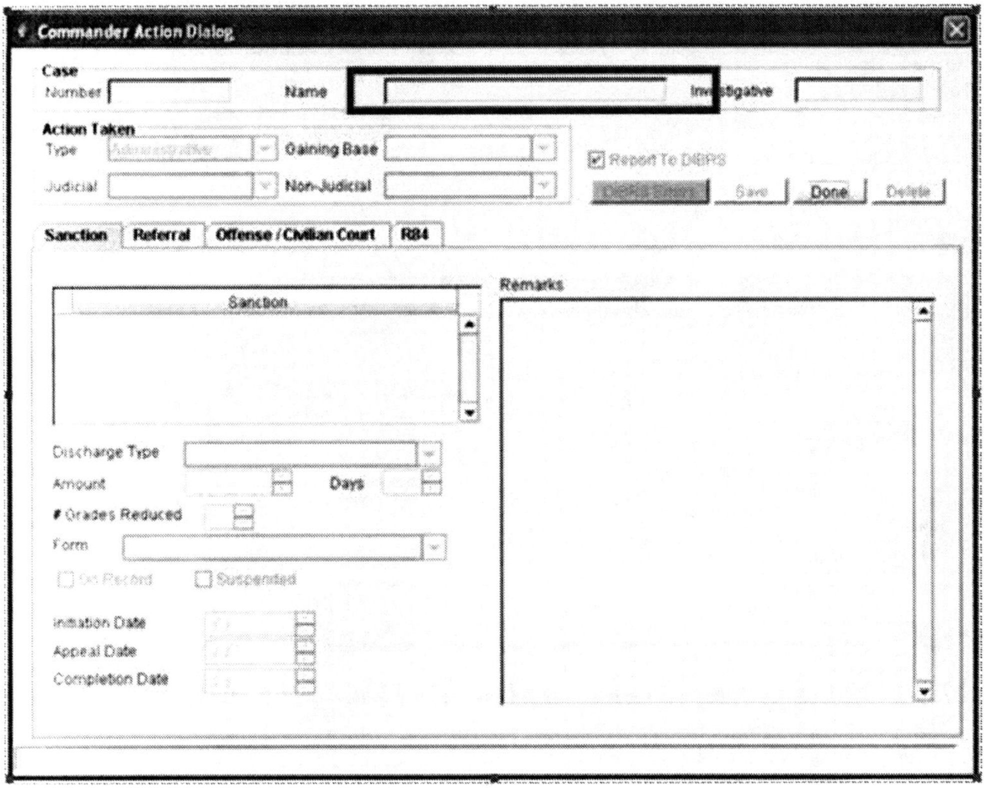

A2.2.19. **F556** *Missing required Offense segment for this Incident*

Figure A2.17. Offense.

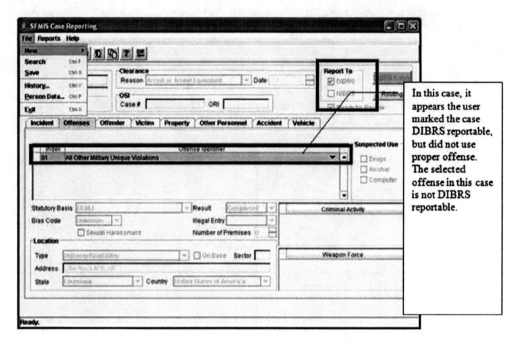

A2.2.20. **F589** *Type Weapon/Force Used is required because this Incident is a suicide*

A2.2.20.1. Users must indicate the Weapon/Force used by the subject.

Figure A2.18. Weapon Used.

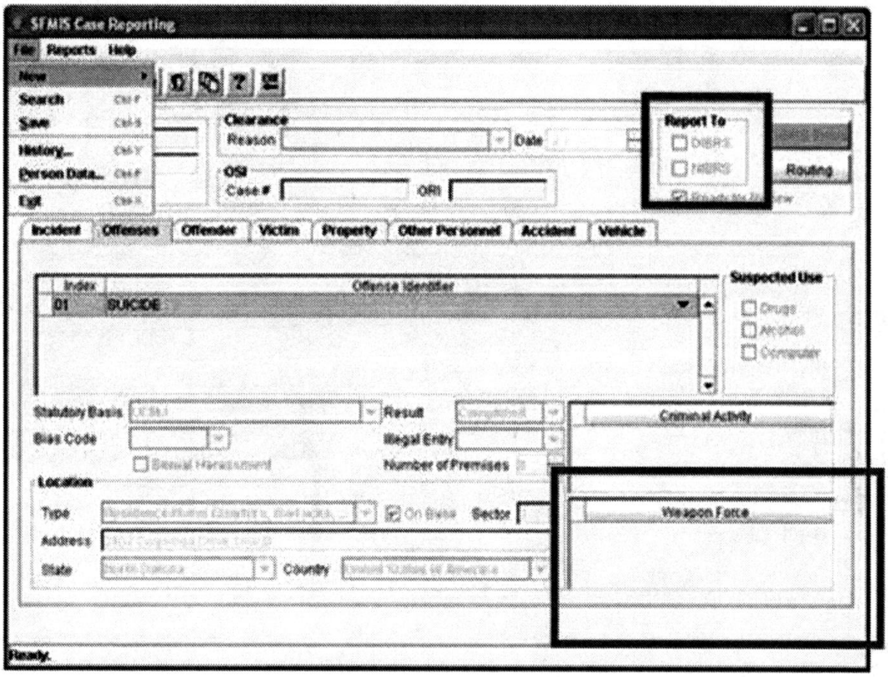

A2.2.21. **F677** *Warning: Type of Weapon/Force Used is required but was not reported -- recoding to "95" for NIBRS*

Figure A2.19. Weapons Used.

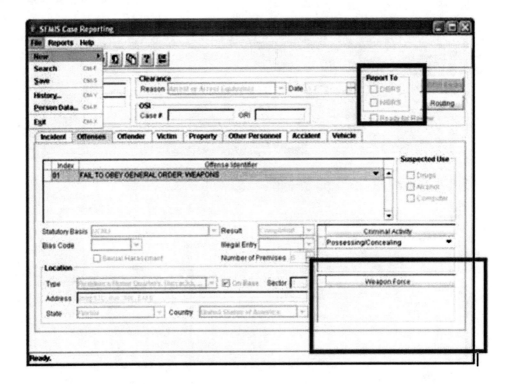

A2.2.22. **M751** *Missing arrestee information which is required to send B Offense to NIBRS*

A2.2.22.1. Ensure you use the correct offense. Circumstances affect the offense which you select. An incident where damage to a vehicle has occurred may be considered "damage to private property" unless an offender is apprehended.

A2.2.23. **P541** *Drug information is not allowed unless Property Loss by is 6 and Property Description is 10*

A2.2.23.1. Drug information cannot be entered unless it identified as drugs (description is 10) and the property is seized (Property Loss Code 6).

Figure A2.20. Seizure Information.

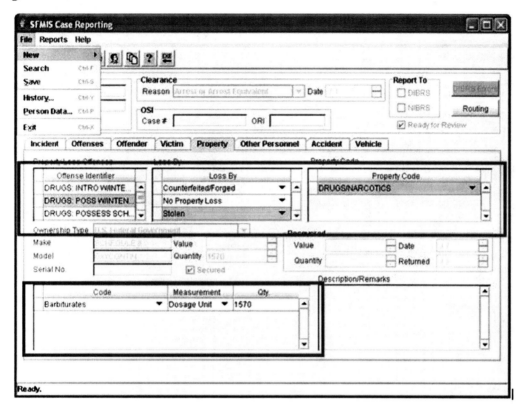

A2.2.24. **P590** *Quantity cannot be reported if Property is Drugs/Narcotics, Money, or Neg/Non-Neg Instruments*

Figure A2.21. Amount.

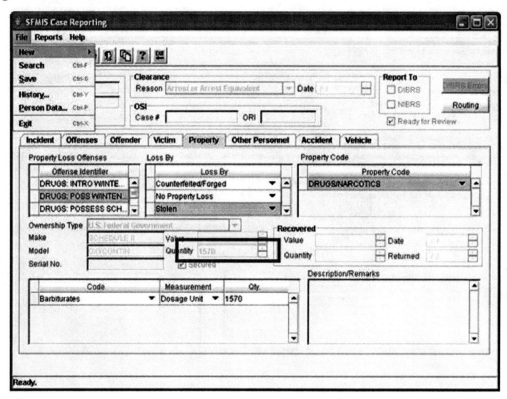

A2.2.25. **R514** *Transaction attempted to process a segment for which no parent incident (segment M) exists*

A2.2.25.1. This error message informs the user when SFMIS attempts to submit an administrative segment which there is no longer a case report for. This is most likely caused by different record retention periods required by the USAF and DMDC. SFMIS maintains case reports for five years, at which time the records are purged as required by the Air Force Records Management System (AFRIMS), unless Brady Law or other requirements apply. DMDC does not have a purge requirement at this time. These differences cause these types of errors which may require manual correction by the SFMIS Program Management Office (PMO). Before referring these incidents to the PMO ensure that all confinement records are tied to an incident report.

A2.2.26. **R789** *Report Date should not be before Arrest/Apprehension Date*

Figure A2.22. Incident Received.

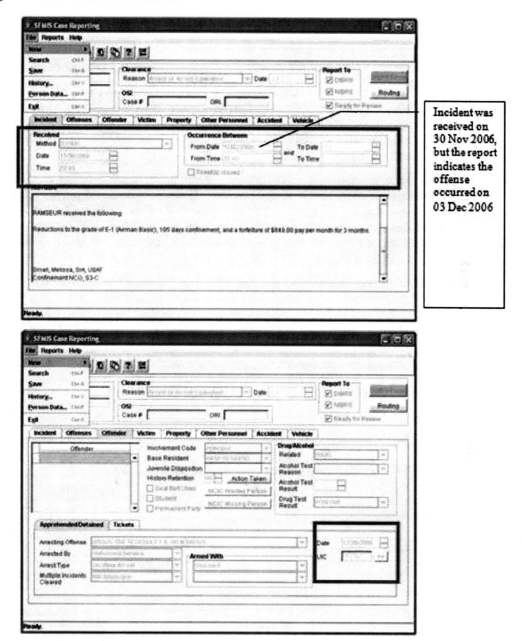

A2.2.27. **R792** *Warning: No Offense (in Results of Trial) which allows cross check with Corrections for Sex Offender Processing Required*

A2.2.27.1. Reported by AMJAMS, refers to SFMIS and AMJAMS data not matching at DMDC.

A2.2.28. R817 *Personal information (last name, first name) in Correction does not match Offender/Arrestee.*

A2.2.28.1. Ensure the names in the case report match the confinement module. This may happen due to letters being transposed, or name changes due to marriage or divorces.

A2.2.29. V597 *UCMJ Code 134-U7 should not be used -- use the Offense Code for the offense solicited instead*

A2.2.29.1. When reporting incidents to DIBRS do not select the offense "Solicitation" instead, use the offense which was solicited. The person that performed the act should be listed in the offender tab as "Principal" and the offender which asked them to perform the offense is the "Solicitor."

A2.2.29.2. **As a reminder, our reporting system is incident based, not offender based.** Please remember, that if more than one offense occurred, and not all offenders were involved separate case reports need to be generated. This is not due to how SFMIS is designed, but due to the DIBRS/NIBRS (National Incident Based Reporting System) records incidents. A lot of valuable information in how case reports should be handled is included in the DIBRS manual.

A2.2.30. V716 *Warning: Injury Type for this Victim is required but was not reported -- recoding to "N" for NIBRS*

Figure A2.23. Injury.

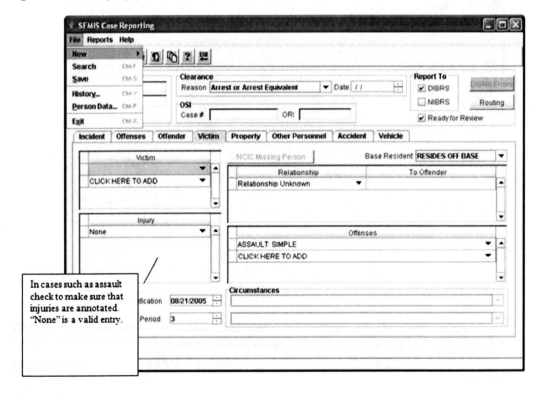

A2.2.31. **V734** *Offender Related to this Victim is required if non-"00" Offenders exist for the current Incident*

Figure A2.24. VWAP.

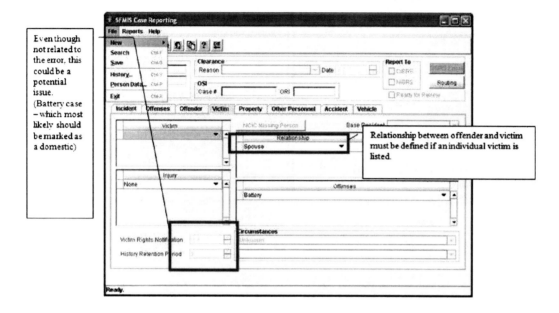

A2.2.32. **V742** *If Offense is 11A or 36B, Sex of Victim and Offender must be different in at least one case*

A2.2.32.1. 11A Forcible Rape (Except Statutory Rape)

A2.2.32.1.1. **Definition:** The carnal knowledge of a person, forcibly and/or against that person's will or not forcibly or against the person's will in instances where the victim is incapable of giving consent because of his/her temporary or permanent mental or physical incapacity. *Note*: If force was used or threatened, the crime should be classified as Forcible Rape regardless of the age of the victim. If no force was used or threatened and the victim was under the statutory age of consent, the crime should be classified as Statutory Rape.

A2.2.32.2. 36B Statutory Rape

A2.2.32.2.1. **Definition:** Non-forcible sexual intercourse with a person who is under the statutory age of consent. **Note:** If force was used or threatened, the offense should be classified as Forcible Rape not Statutory Rape.

Figure A2.25. Gender.

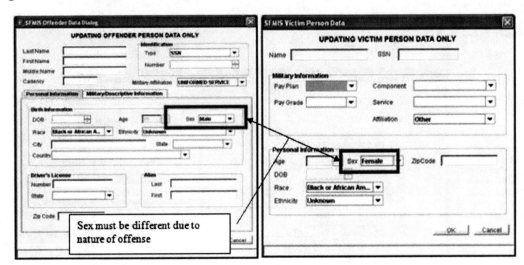

CPSIA information can be obtained at www.ICGtesting.com
Printed in the USA
BVOW05s1049140115
383280BV00014B/191/P